MIND THAT CHILD!

a casebook on the controversy
over standards in primary education

Tom Kitwood & Marie Macey

Writers and Readers Publishing Cooperative

Published 1977 by Writers and Readers Publishing Cooperative, 14 Talacre
Road, London NW5 3PE

Printed by The Trade Printing Company, 14 Sun Street, London EC2.

The Confederation for the Advancement of State Education originated in
a protest against inadequate accommodation at a Cambridge primary school
in 1960. In 1962 the national committee was formed. There are now 78
local associations. Members are parents and teachers and others with an
interest in education in this country.

CASE works for three main objectives:
1. To collect and spread information on education, through meetings,
newsletters, study groups, guide booklets and advice services on all kinds of
local and national issues.
2. To press for improvements in the education service, closer links between
the community and schools and a fully comprehensive education system
which would offer the widest possible opportunities for every child.
3. To further understanding and cooperation between teachers and parents,
through greater participation by parents, more parents offering voluntary
assistance to teachers, more parent/teacher organisations, and better
conditions of work for teachers.

To know more about CASE, to find out about an association in your area,
or to apply for membership, write to
Yvonne Peecock, 10 Parkfield Street, Rowhedge, Colchester, Essex
Tel: 020-628519

Contents

Preface

This booklet has a simple message, one which is very relevant to our current predicament in education and national life. In essence, it is this. In order to evaluate any piece of educational research one must have a conception of what education is for; and in order to understand what education is for one must have a conception of society, as it has been, as it is and as it might be. Seen in this way the controversy over standards in education takes on a new significance.

The publication of the report from Lancaster University on Teaching Styles and Pupil Progress sparked off a good deal more than the somewhat slanted public comment so widely quoted by the media. In the minds of those who tend to reflect and consider rather than react instantaneously, questions were posed anew. To many of us in the Confederation for the Advancement of State Education the claims of some commentators that at last it was now *"scientifically proved"* that 'progressive' teaching methods were inferior and that the well tried 'traditional' methods were best, were far from convincing. Indeed the very notion of polarising teaching styles in this manner appeared a most unrealistic attitude.

CASE was concerned to make the kind of contribution to public debate the situation demanded. They saw the need for a brief and clear examination of the underlying issues. Such an examination the authors have certainly achieved. Although the views expressed are in no way a statement in part or whole of CASE policy they are views CASE believes should have the widest possible readership.

This is not merely a critique of a particular piece of

research. It is far more constructive and encouraging than that, for here something positive is said. There is a well deserved assumption that contemporary education is achieving results of value to society as a whole; there is also a warning that society should beware a narrowing of the criteria on which such judgements are made.

I am grateful for this opportunity to thank Tom Kitwood, Marie Macey and the Writers and Readers Publishing Cooperative for their generosity and cooperation in bringing this CASEbook to fruition.

Jim Winstone, Chairman,
National Committee, Confederation for the
Advancement of State Education.

January 1977.

1. Spotlight on the Primary School

These are ominous days for education. For the last few years there have been many warning signs, in both scholarly and popular writing, and in the public discussion of educational issues. If changes are brought about, it may be under a smokescreen of irrelevant propaganda, false argument, and appeal to vested interests. And no doubt, when the time comes for action, all measures will be justified by reference to those two gods which seem to dominate the present life of Britain — the demands of industry and the need for strict economy. It seems likely that many people who do not understand the issues sufficiently clearly will be misled, and find themselves supporting policies to which they would be strongly opposed if only they realised the consequences. These changes may amount to a swindle which could affect the children who are now at school, and those of many years to come. We are all involved, because the issue concerns the kind of world we wish to live in, and our responsibility to hand on a humane society to the rising generation.

The central issue is that of standards in education; closely related are the questions of what we should teach our children, and by what methods. Some of the most heated argument surrounds the primary schools where it has been alleged that standards are falling, with disastrous effects on the education that follows. Now, it is claimed, the situation is so serious that many of those who finally emerge from their schooling are neither qualified nor fitted for a productive and responsible place in society. Naturally, the confidence of many teachers is being undermined as criticism of their work, often done under conditions which are far from ideal, becomes more outspoken. We may well soon reach the situation in which neither parents nor teachers feel that they know what is best for the children. It is not surprising that there is a general loss of nerve, and with it a tendency to rush to any remedies that are proposed, regardless of whether these may prove to be futile and short-sighted.

We want to explain briefly, but as clearly as we can, what we believe to be the issues lying behind this debate. If you are a practising teacher of any kind, or a parent of a child at school, you will appreciate that this is a far from trivial matter. It may, however, be of even greater significance than you realised, or than the media have implied. You may feel inclined to leave the whole question to the 'experts'; actually, expert knowledge is not required in order to understand it, as we hope to show. You may find yourself in disagreement with our conclusions, but we hope that you will be able to see the problem more clearly, and have the information necessary for holding a considered opinion. The word of the 'experts', in this as in other matters, may well be untrustworthy, and we would do well to judge for ourselves. In the long run, the survival of democracy requires that we do so when issues such as this are in debate.

Perhaps you remember the great wave of criticism of current educational practice which came with the Black Papers. The fifth of these, published in 1975, describes comprehensive schools as a 'disaster'; universities as places of general disrepute; roundly criticises the 'progressive bandwagon' for 'damage being inflicted on young lives', and sets out to enable the reader to 'oppose dangerous fashions which have corrupted many in the teaching profession'. Because of the widespread publicity which was given to them, the Black Papers created a great deal of anxiety among teachers, policy-makers, and perhaps most of all among parents, who are naturally concerned for their children's prospects.

Those who were in a position to understand the problems in a wider context were, however, generally more wary. For the Black Papers had one redeeming feature: they were so blatantly dishonest, offensive and narrow in their outlook that they were unlikely to cause much alarm to those educationalists who actually read them properly. After all, who can take seriously any supposedly academic publication which uses so many emotive slogans, contains so few verified (or verifiable) facts, and which argues — apparently in complete seriousness — that children can be divided into sheep and goats!

Since 1975 the general concern about our schools has continued to grow. There has been talk about a national core curriculum, about the possibility of more rigorous testing — supported, as always, by the cry for 'adequately' trained personnel in the manufacturing industries. Mr. Callaghan took the unusual step as Prime Minister in making a major speech on the subject; and Dr. Rhodes Boyson was reported as suggesting the use of tests to decide which teachers to sack for inefficiency. It seems probable that educational standards will be the topic of many heated (and often misinformed) debates, both in parliament and elsewhere, for some time to come. As a nation facing crises of several kinds, we are in a mood of self-criticism. It is understandable and appropriate that we should submit our educational system, on which we spend about £6,000 million per year, to very careful scrutiny.

In May 1976 a spotlight was shone on the primary sector of education, shaking confidence in the system even more seriously than before. This came in the form of a report from Lancaster University — *Teaching Styles and Pupil Progress*. The findings of this inquiry are presented in the name of science; that is, supposedly objective, unbiased knowledge, based on accurate observation and measurement. The 'Bennett Report', as it came to be called, resonated with the misgivings that were already being felt. The story quickly spread that it has now been *proved, scientifically*, that 'progressive' methods of teaching are inferior, and that the old tried ways are best.

Much was made of the report by politicians with axes to grind, and of course it was taken up by the media, including national television. In the newspapers it gave rise to such headlines as "Demand Return to Three R's, Parents Told", and "People or Guinea Pigs in Class?", to give two examples from the *Yorkshire Post*. Not only was it regarded as excellent news value by the popular press, however; even the editor of the *Times Educational Supplement* was prepared to commit himself by writing in *The Times*, on the day that the report was published: "Now for the first time there is a piece of solid research which measures the progress of pupils under different types of classroom regime and comes up with clear and uncompromising findings". Here, we believe, even a notable educationalist was in error.

Little can be done in the short term to change the dominant impression which the report has made on the general public, most of whom will not have read it for themselves. The crucial question now to be settled is how it will influence the thinking of the educational community: politicians and policy-makers, those who are involved in teacher education, practising teachers, and the group which is numerically by far the strongest — the parents themselves. We believe that the issues involved are very significant and far-reaching, going miles beyond the apparently simple question of how children are taught in the primary school classrooms. They could affect the whole future of our children, and beyond that the kind of society we are creating for ourselves; perhaps, indirectly, whether the end of the twentieth century in Britain is to be marked by democracy or tyranny, freedom or oppression. It is important that we try to understand this question as clearly as we can.

Almost inevitably this booklet will be taken by those who do not read it carefully as a defence of 'progressive' teaching styles — whatever that term is meant to indicate. So at the outset we must state that this is not our aim. Any thoughtful person involved in education, who knows something about the various fads, fancies, and bandwagons of pedagogic thought during this century, would want to be more cautious. One simply cannot make blanket statements of approval or condemnation. We believe the sound approach involves looking very carefully — and critically — at the whole range of educational thought, and trying to discover what may be helpful and relevant in each new emphasis, in particular contexts. Also it is necessary to remember that each outstanding teacher develops a style that is unique and personal. One can make recommendations, but there are no standard formulae for success.

We must also emphasise that we share in the general concern about high standards in Reading, Arithmetic and English. This booklet is in no way an attempt to question their rightness as educational aims. However, we recognise that they are not the only elements involved in a sound primary education. Creativity, freedom of expression, individuality of thought, social confidence, practical understanding, and physical development are significant, too. It is misleading to imply that a concern for these is in conflict with the more 'academic' requirements.

We are advocating standards which, far from being lower, are in fact considerably higher than those for which the Black Paper pressure groups have been campaigning.

So our position cannot be given a crude label such as 'traditional' or 'progressive'; most people who have given careful thought to educational issues would say the same though they may differ in the aspects which they emphasise. One of the worst outcomes of the debate about standards, and one of the ways in which the Bennett Report is most seriously unscientific, is that a sharp division between two rival approaches to education has been implied. So please do not interpret this booklet as an uncritical plea for something called 'progressive education'.

We want, rather, to set the debate in its wider context. The survival of such democracy as we have requires a large body of informed opinion when so much hangs in the balance.

2. The Controversy in its Historical Context

Before we can make a proper judgement on the question of standards, we need to understand the recent changes in our educational system against a background of some 200 years or more. In this perspective it would be very naive to suggest that we should now, in effect, put the clock back 20 years (which, it seems, is what some politicians would wish). The larger historical context is an important but much neglected aspect of any debate such as this. It is, indeed, a vital part of all educational research.

The first thing to make clear is that we have not adopted the methods which we are currently using, especially some of those which might count as 'progressive', in an irresponsible way. There have been many pointers that something very much better was possible than what 'traditional' education, at its worst, was doing. For well over a century it has been recognised that under some circumstances, teachers and pupils can be working on the same side, rather than as enemies who hated one another. It has been discovered that in an atmosphere of trust and acceptance children can be given more freedom and responsibility than was previously believed; when this is brought about, the more brutal forms of discipline are not needed. In some of the great private ventures of education it has been demonstrated that when the climate is one of caring, when basic human needs are met, learning and development can occur to an unimagined extent even in children judged severely subnormal. We are now so used to such insights that we are inclined to forget how novel they are in educational thought.

It is not only from the brave and imaginative work of educational pioneers that indications of better ways have come. There have been other pointers, too, that we could do something more constructive than sit children in rows for several hours each day, and impart what adults count as 'knowledge'. Much careful work, both with normal and retarded children, has led to a deeper understanding of the development of the human mind. We realise that learning is an active process. We know something of how children develop in stages, and at various speeds. We recognise that those who are hungry, tired, anxious or hostile, cannot learn. We are beginning to understand why it is that some children, whose faculties are sound, are turned by 'the system' into failures, while others with similar capacities become successes. Although, of course, there have been mistakes, there has been a serious attempt to apply such insights to what we do in primary schools. Anyone whose educational thinking takes no account of this lacks both knowledge and compassion.

Negatively, too, there has been much ground for dissatisfaction with what 'traditional' education has achieved for the population as a whole. For example, the 'teddy boys' of the 50's and the 'mods and rockers' of the 60's emerged from schools which had signally failed to help them. The existence of 2 million or so subliterate adults in Great Britain is not the consequence of progressive education. The long history of strife between different sectors of the community, which has a considerable relevance to the crises we now face in our industry and economy, is the story of those who have prospered, and those who have suffered, under the old-style educational system.

Taking this further, it is not too far-fetched to

remember that those who engaged in two world wars —
on both sides — were the products of 'traditional'
education. The force of this comment applies especially
to the leaders and decision-makers, who were almost all
from the educationally privileged classes. It was they
who directed the annihilation of 6 million Jews, and
who ordered the destruction of communities of
civilians. It would be false, of course, to lay the blame
directly or entirely on their education; there have
always been humane and generous-minded teachers,
even within a system that worked against their aims.
There is ground, however, for thinking that these allied
sicknesses of the human spirit — the urge to dominate
and the urge to submit to domination — are closely
related to the way people were taught and trained as
children. To process human beings so that they
mechanically obey orders, and use their skills without
thought for what they are doing, is to pave the way for
tyranny in society as a whole.

If we take a look further back at the history of
education in this country, it is not an impressive picture
which emerges. It would seem highly unlikely that what
we have inherited from the past, its harshness softened
here and there, its more blatant injustices varnished
over, would be a fitting instrument for the children of
today. Yet Britain is in a position of unparalleled
educational opportunity. We have the possibility for
doing something much better than we have ever done
before, if only we have the nerve to ensure that it is
carried through. But for this we must see clearly what
we are about.

One factor which tends to be forgotten is that
schools have been open to all in Britain for only just
over a century. Prior to this, there is a haphazard record
of education which can be traced back to the sixth

century, almost all of it geared to the requirements of minorities — priests, aristocracy, and later the rising middle class. The majority of the population were not deemed in need of systematic schooling. Among the first attempts to rectify this were the Charity School movement of the seventeenth century and the Sunday Schools of the late eighteenth, both of which were aimed, in some sense, at the 'moral rescue' of the poor. Around 1800, not only was universal education opposed as a matter of principle, but even subjects such as writing and arithmetic were judged unnecessary — even harmful — for the working population.

It was only in the late nineteenth century that a national system of elementary schooling became established, with the aim of providing for the supposed needs of the whole population. By the time 'education for all' did come into being, there were already deeply rooted patterns of thinking about the relation between the person, the school, work and society. To put it very crudely — people were to be educated for their station in life. The aim for the majority was to turn out a social character, well trained in habits of regularity, self-restraint, obedience and hard work.

Education served a political purpose also. Industrialisation was far advanced; the working classes had been given the vote; the trade unions were growing in strength, adopting their own methods of self-help and education. Those who were in power turned to the notion of universal education partly out of fear; they justified their legislation in terms of the need for a responsible (trained) democracy, and the requirement that Britain should have a workforce able to maintain her place as a major industrial power, the head of a large and growing empire.

In this way the educational system which became

established in Britain in the early part of the twentieth century was unbalanced from the start. A set of methods which worked quite well for a middle-class and upper-class minority were assumed to be appropriate for the whole population. Many of the changes which have occurred since then should be understood as minor adjustments to that basic pattern, hopefully aimed at enabling education to be more relevant to all, or at least less obnoxious. It is only very recently that the prospect of a genuinely universal education, designed to serve the needs of all, has become a realistic possibility.

The 1944 Education Act, which appeared to offer the chance of an excellent education to anyone who was bright enough to deserve it, was in many respects a fraud. For it abandoned the earlier notion of inherited social status as the ticket to a good school, and replaced it by that of personal ability. The reality is that by an odd coincidence — totally against the laws of nature — high social status and personal ability (as measured by I.Q.) generally went together! (Even the recent finding that Sir Cyril Burt, whose work on I.Q.'s provided the foundation for the 1944 act, may have been so unscientific as to invent imaginary co-workers and to fake some of his measurements, hardly makes this fact less curious.) The net result was that the Grammar Schools, officially designed so that all would have equal access to their advantages, were almost entirely filled by middle class children.

The existence of the great hurdle of the 11+ exam, after which children were almost irrevocably divided into two main groups, had serious consequences for primary education. Curriculum and teaching methods were almost entirely geared to the short-term objective of passing an examination, which only about 20% were going to pass in any case. The needs of the majority were sacrificed for the sake of a fortunate few, and broader educational aims were often forgotten. All this went right against the recommendations of the Hadow Report of 1931 which, though limited in its scope, did insist that primary education should be thought of in terms of activity and experience rather than rote learning. There are now several million people in their 20's, 30's, and 40's who were educated under this system. If bitterness between classes is a feature of this age-group, their education is partly to blame.

Today, we have largely abolished selection for secondary education; we have raised the school leaving age to 16; there are more places available in universities and colleges, and more opportunities for adult education, than ever before. At last the pressure of short-term objectives is off the primary schools. They are now free, in theory at least, to develop a broader curriculum which can help the development of all children; they do not have to push a minority through an examination. This is the culmination of a movement which has been going on for over a century; it is vital that it does not now lose its momentum.

But the influence of political manoeuvrings cannot be underestimated. In 1965 the Labour Government requested local authorities to reorganise their schools on comprehensive lines (though a year later made it clear that funds would not be provided for the necessary changes). In 1970 the Conservatives adopted a delaying tactic, by effectively having no policy at all. Even now, when the proposals of 1965 have been largely implemented except in a few recalcitrant areas, the position is far from satisfactory. For many of the new comprehensives model themselves on the old grammar schools, just as they, in their turn, tried to imitate the public schools. Many of the new posts of authority are taken by people with a narrowly academic approach, and the sole criterion of a school's 'success' becomes the number of 'O' and 'A' level passes. The old story repeats itself: a system which outwardly appears to be more fair perpetuates the longstanding inequalities.

Despite the achievements of the educational reforms which have been carried through, the cry goes up that standards are falling. It has been heard more loudly during the last year or two, with much encouragement from the media. Comprehensive schools are blamed for the ills of the nation, even before some of them have had time for a single generation of pupils to pass through. The so-called evidence for falling standards is, however, largely illusion, reinforced by anxiety. For example, many ex-grammar school staff are now meeting for the first time boys and girls who had formerly been consigned by the system to secondary modern schools. More children than ever before are working for 'O' and 'A' levels, so naturally the teacher's job is harder. In the physical sciences the level of understanding required for 'A' level is comparable to that of a first degree fifteen years ago (though with a somewhat smaller range of knowledge). And in industry and commerce employers who complain about low standards are apt to forget that the backgrounds of people applying for certain jobs has changed; the boy who used to take an apprenticeship now gets a degree in engineering; the girl who formerly became a secretary now finds that she can go to university. Against any allegations that standards have fallen we must take factors such as these into account, and remember that we now have more people at the higher levels of education than ever before in our history.

Our primary schools were once described as the best comprehensive schools we have, but now they also are being attacked because of an alleged drop in standards. The obsession with testing and measurement is nearing the point of hysteria; there's even talk of 'screening' all children at the age of 5! Perhaps this sad lack of vision, this depressingly inadequate conception of what education is about, comes because those who make these complaints are themselves the products of a deficient educational system. Processed by the conveyor belt of exams, they expect everyone else to be like them.

They believe in the infallibility of formal, 'objective' tests much more than do the psychologists who design them.

British education has certainly had a chequered history, as even this brief sketch makes clear. The remarkable fact is how much progress has been made. If we continue true to the best we know, learning from mistakes and benefitting from new insights, we have the potential to set an example in education to the whole world. We could create a more just and harmonious society, adapted to the conditions of the end of the twentieth century.

Resources may be scarce, and hours of work less, but the chance to be fully human may be widely available as it has not been since the industrial revolution. It would be a sad day if we were now to revert to a mechanical system which confers educational advantage on a minority, thereby sacrificing the rest on the altar of 'standards'. Considering the vested interests involved, and the prevailing social and political climate, the dangers of this are real. This is the wider context against which the claims of the Bennett Report are to be judged.

3. The Claims of Recent Research

Educational policy, like all social policy, has generally been justified by reference to some sort of research. It cannot be claimed, however, that policy decisions have ever been made on the basis, or as a result, of research. They seem to be much more a consequence of political will (and power), and/or a response to change which is already under way. The major Education Acts illustrate this clearly, for they were all passed to legitimate changes which were in progress, and they utilized selected 'evidence' for the same purpose.

Now, at a time when Britain is labouring under enormous economic and social problems, including galloping inflation, massive unemployment (including teachers and graduates), increasing vandalism, violence, alcoholism and stress-based illnesses, an inquiry has been initiated into educational standards. And while a concern about how well our educational system is functioning is neither new nor misguided, its current intensity and particular thrust are both. At a time when we have more people with high qualifications than ever before, there is something fundamentally illogical in complaining that academic standards are falling; even more in implying that a major responsibility for this lies with the primary school.

The piece of research which has provided the necessary 'evidence' to support a move to implement the routine testing of children on a national scale, to reinstate 'traditional' methods of teaching and to formalize curriculum content, is the report from Lancaster University — *Teaching Styles and Pupil*

Progress. The reason for the heavy reliance on this particular piece of research appears to be due far more to the fact that it is the only currently available report which produces the kind of evidence desired by certain politicians, than by its status as research per se. Nevertheless, because the 'Bennett Report' makes strong claims to have proved, objectively, that 'modern methods' lead to loss of academic standards, we must see what, precisely, was involved in this highly controversial study.

The research began with an analysis of the ideas of 'traditional' or 'formal' and 'progressive' or 'informal'. This was done partly through an examination of some of the background literature, and partly on the basis of asking teachers how they understood the concepts. Various components of each 'style' were then put into the form of a questionnaire, which was completed by 468 primary school teachers in North West England. The questions covered such aspects of their work as classroom layout, method of handling the curriculum, freedom or control in pupils' work, testing and grading, and methods of exerting discipline. Some aspects of teaching which might be judged as highly relevant were not included, however; one example is the question of whether the teacher gave pupils feedback about their work in some form other than marking.

The answers to the questionnaire were processed by a computer. A very elegant and fairly new statistical technique called cluster analysis was used; this has a strong artistic appeal, but is notorious for giving a variety of results depending on the programme which is chosen. As a result, 12 clusters of teachers emerged, each with similar characteristics as 'measured' by the questionnaire. Here a straightforward 'impression-judgement' was made, so as to arrange the 12 clusters along a spectrum from highly 'formal' to highly 'informal'. From this stage forward in the research the 'formal-informal' division was used: such finer points as, say, being 'formal' in discipline and 'informal' in classroom layout, or having a tightly planned curriculum in one subject and a flexible one in another, were of necessity ignored because of the nature of the method.

For the next stage of the research 37 teachers were selected, divided into 3 groups to represent either extreme and the middle of the formal-informal continuum. The 'personalities' of their pupils were investigated by questionnaires, using such variables as sociability, contentiousness, anxiety, motivation, neuroticism, psychoticism, and fidget/distractibility. The pupils' initial attainment levels and progress over a year, were measured by means of standard tests; their creative writing was examined by getting them to write a 'descriptive' and an 'imaginative' story.

The final stage of the inquiry involved making observations of a 10% sample of the pupils in the classroom. Their behaviour was recorded and categorised under various headings. For example 'work activity' included ruling lines and queueing to see the teacher; 'interaction' included attracting attention and nudging; 'avoidance' included gazing into space, or out of the window; and 'movement' included fidgeting, scratching, shuffling, playing with hair.

A mass of data emerged from this very painstaking and exacting piece of research. By far the most controversial of the findings was that pupils in 'informal' classrooms had apparently made less progress than those who had been taught in 'formal' settings, the differences being equivalent to the kind of progress which might be expected over about 3—5 months. The crux of the whole report was 3 small graphs which appeared to show, as clearly as any measurements made in a physics laboratory, that in the case of Reading, Mathematics and English the informal classes had substantially worse results.

This was partially achieved by the way the slopes on the graph were drawn!

One other finding which attracted wide attention was that very good results, and the highest gains of all in one subject area, occurred in the class of a moderately 'informal' teacher. The report was honest in drawing attention to this, but made little reference to it in the concluding chapter. Here, despite the modest tone of the writing, very emphatic claims were made about the inferences to be drawn from the research. Bennett effectively claimed that since there is no doubt that informal methods of teaching result in lower pupil attainment, we should now call for a reappraisal of progressive education and a closer examination of teacher training. It is not surprising, then, that the report created such a stir, coinciding with a mood of general despondency in education. Around the same time a piece of research carried out in the South of England, along rather similar lines, was reported. This quickly vanished from public consciousness, perhaps because it pointed to.very different conclusions.

The Bennett Report epitomizes a particular research tradition which has dominated social research (including that into educational issues). We are suggesting that it is not so much this particular piece of research, but the validity of the whole approach which is seriously open to question. Yet many claims are made on the basis of its 'findings' — some of which have affected the course of millions of lives. For this reason alone, it is worth taking a careful look at what generally passes for 'educational research'. For some highly significant lessons can be drawn from this — not least important of which concern the role played by so-called 'scientific' activities in the planning of society.

4. The Failure of a Method

When we take the long-term history of education in Britain into account, and face seriously the human prospect of the next 20 or 30 years, it is clear that the apparently small matter of teaching styles is part of a much larger issue. It is certainly not one which can be settled by a single piece of research. For we have not yet had time to settle down after a period of many changes, or gained sufficient practical knowledge to modify our teacher education. We would probably need to wait for a whole generation, until there were parents, too, who had been educated by new methods, before we could make a fair assessment. So whatever conclusions are drawn from particular pieces of research at this time, they could not form sufficient ground for a wholesale reversal of policies.

If serious account is taken of both the aims of education, and of the historical background, we would contend that there are good grounds for believing that we have been moving in the right direction.

Nevertheless, it is worth taking a careful look at what generally passes for 'educational research', because some very significant lessons can be drawn from it. During the last 20 years or so the systematic study of education has used up a large amount of time, money, and talent: this is well justified in a topic so vital to our national well-being. But educational research has been dominated by one particular kind of approach, whose validity is seriously open to question. Since many claims are made on the basis of its 'findings', it is worth explaining it in more detail.

The method of inquiry seems to be modelled on the physics of the late nineteenth century: that is, it assumes that there is an objective educational reality which exists apart from the way it is perceived by those who are involved in it. The task, then, is to take numerical measurements, just as one would measure mass, length and time. The data obtained in this way is, granted certain conditions, stated to be 'reliable' and 'valid'. Through it the researcher is supposed to be able to understand what is going on, or at least to be able to predict what will happen under certain sets of conditions. This is what is usually meant by 'scientific' educational research. Since the arrival of the computer the number of measurements that can be processed simultaneously has, of course, enormously increased, and with that, the 'scientific' status of the enterprise. The Bennett Report is a test case of the soundness of this approach, since it is such a good example of it, and in a highly controversial case.

This style of research has had a long history, one of its principal roots being the study of I.Q.'s, which goes back to the turn of the century. Then during World War II methods which were already in existence were greatly extended, and they had many uses. Among these were the selection of people for appropriate places in the forces; the elimination from combat of those who might break down under stress; the inculcation of loyalty to leaders; and in general the formation of a disciplined, well-motivated, fighting corps. Further developments in method occurred during the wars in Korea and Vietnam, while there was a widespread transfer of research skills to such fields as advertising, selling and education.

All this might make one cautious about accepting the results of educational research. In general, though, these origins have been forgotten, and it has come to be accepted by many educationalists that this is the right way of making inquiry into teaching and learning. There is, however, no general agreement among social scientists that this is a valid way to carry out investigations in such a delicate area. Indeed, it has been suggested by several critics that the commitment of educational research to this style of inquiry is fundamentally mistaken. For example, the method reveals nothing about the actual processes which are involved; it fails to comprehend people's thoughts and feelings; and the whole business of treating people as if they were passively responding to various kinds of 'treatment' (e.g. 'formal' or 'informal' teaching) is unsuited for the study of teaching and learning, which are thoroughly active processes, for pupils as well as teachers. In short, such methods cannot be dissociated from their military and para-military uses, where they were geared to the processing of people who had very little say in what would happen to them.

There is a somewhat sick logic in applying such research methods to education. For their origins lay in the desire to differentiate people on a variety of grounds. And the function of testing in education has remained, fundamentally, that of division and separation. *It has an uncanny tendency to reinforce the status quo.*

Just suppose, however, that we were to accept the technique as valid. It would be necessary to analyse the primary school situation into a number of 'variables', each of which might possibly have an influence on the learning process. We could put these into 5 main groups: those connected with the wider social and historical context (A), the school (B), the teacher (C), the teaching and learning process (D), and the pupil (E). The highly simplified analysis given here yields 40 variables, though some of them would have to be broken down a good deal further before they could be 'measured'. We might end up with about 100 variables each of which, if the researcher were sufficiently ingenious, could be turned into numbers. If the layout of the scheme shown below reminds you of a driving licence application this is no coincidence; there also the information is treated as a set of variables, to be processed by a computer.

							Variable No.
A Context							
Type of country	...	...	...	...	...	...	1
Educational history	...	...	...	...	...	...	2
Government educational policy	...	...	...	...	...	3
Funds allocated to primary education	...	...	...	4
B School							
Type of school	...	...	...	...	...	...	5
Type of area ...	...	...	...	...	...	...	6
Policy of local authority	...	...	...	...	...	7
Policy and power of head teacher	...	...	...	8 9
Climate of opinion among staff	...	...	...	...	10
C Teacher							
Age, sex, social class	...	...	...	...	...	11 12 13
Character, temperament	...	...	...	...	...	14 15
Aptitude for teaching, liking for children, commitment to the job	...	...	...	16 17 18
Experience, beliefs about the work of a teacher	...	19 20
D Teaching and Learning							
Subject being taught	...	...	...	...	...	21
Mode of organisation of the curriculum	...	...	...	22
Type of classroom layout	...	...	...	...	...	23
Method of marking and of commenting on children's work	...	...	...	...	24 25
Means of keeping discipline	...	...	...	...	26
Resources, in the form of equipment, books, visual aids, etc	...	...	...	...	...	27
E Pupil							
Age, sex, social class	...	...	...	...	...	28 29 30
Character, temperament	...	...	...	...	...	31 32
Aptitude for learning, liking for the teacher, commitment to school work	...	...	...	...	33 34 35
Extent of parental encouragement	...	...	...	36
Friends in and out of class	...	...	...	...	37 38
Whether hungry, tired, anxious	...	...	...	...	39 40

If nothing else, a scheme such as this makes it very plain that the real situation is extremely complex. A piece of research which properly fulfilled the requirements of this view of what it is to be scientific would, of course, have to deal with all the variables. It would need to vary them systematically, control for them, or carry out an extremely elaborate piece of statistical juggling (called 'multivariate analysis') with the computer. No important variable could be ignored.

We can now see the research carried out by the Lancaster team in sharper focus. They have missed out all the context, school and teacher variables, and taken only a few of those to do with pupils. The most controversial measurements were made with a small number of the 'teaching and learning' variables, together with estimates of 'progress' as conventionally defined. The research took no account of many factors which may be highly relevant; it also mixed up some of those it did include, by making the almost meaningless variable of 'teaching style'.

It is easy now to understand the significance of the criticisms of the Bennett Report which have been made by those who believe the method to be fundamentally sound. These have generally focused on the omission of certain variables (e.g. pupils' social class); the method of obtaining particular measurements (e.g. pupil progress); or on the statistical techniques (e.g. the choice of programme for cluster analysis). Each critic has his own concerns and hobby-horses, related perhaps to his own research, and is therefore apt to notice particular kinds of deficiency. But what no-one seems to have observed is that individual criticisms are but a very small sample of those which could have been made if a full scheme of variables had been drawn up. The list of complaints might then have gone on almost indefinitely.

All this raises the question whether such research is worth carrying out at all. This inquiry, which investigated the relationship between a very small number out of the total possible range of variables, and ignored the rest, was a major piece of work. It took 4 years to complete and cost somewhere in the region of 10 to 100 thousand pounds, the figure varying according to which items are counted as costs of the study. A thorough investigation which came nearer to fulfilling the self-imposed standards of this kind of 'science', might take the same team 50 years to complete and cost as much as the nation's annual primary education budget!

It seems, then, that an inquiry such as that carried out by the Lancaster team is bound to be incomplete. Time, money, and human ability are limited in their availability. How then, is it that some, out of all the possible variables, but not others, are chosen for study when research such as this is undertaken? The answer is that it is a haphazard process. In some cases, a particular technique has novel or artistic appeal; sometimes it is simply that certain variables are more easy to measure than others; and often the researcher just draws on his own common sense knowledge, which may be far from scientific. The general rule, to put it crudely, is 'measure what you can, and forget about the rest'.

It is, perhaps, invidious to fasten in this way on a single inquiry in the 'measurement' tradition. Because so much capital was made of it, however, and because of its focal place in recent controversy, it is important to understand what was involved in this piece of research. In fact, Bennett's work has been criticised in a much more crushing way by others than ourselves, and we recognize that his team did attempt to bring humanity and realism into its work by making detailed classroom observations. The Lancaster Report is a recent product of a long tradition in research; it is really this tradition, rather than a particular example, which needs to be reappraised.

The consequences of attempting to study the human

being divorced from a social context by means of simple tests are serious. Even if one accepts that measurement is legitimate in certain areas, we must face the fact that no major piece of research can handle all the relevant variables, and in this sense is bound to distort understanding. In the case of teaching styles, for example, it now seems that our appreciation of the whole issue is more confused than it was before. Highly dubious notions such as 'formal', 'informal', and 'progress' have been over-simplified and made concrete. What is probably worse, the deeply rooted conception of schools as conveyor belts, mechanically providing knowledge and skills to passive people, has now been strengthened. And because the research has been given the prestigious label of 'science', any false impressions it has conveyed may be harder to remove.

Similar considerations apply in other controversial areas. It has been claimed, for example, that mental sickness (or a tendency towards it) can be measured, and the result is that we are in danger of giving 'treatment' to almost anyone who deviates far from the standard conception of what a human being should be, or how he should act. It has been claimed that criminal tendencies are inherited, despite the fact that the most crucial variables, related to a person's expectations and perceptions of what others are thinking, cannot be measured. It has been claimed that black people are less intelligent, as a race, than white; those who have carried out the most elaborate calculations, controlling for every variable they judge to be relevant, such as social class, living conditions and educational opportunity, still have overlooked what is perhaps the most relevant variable of all — the experience of being black in a white people's world with 200 years of submission in one's culture.

New light on the whole question of measurement has come with recent findings about Sir Cyril Burt whose research on intelligence dominated British thought on this topic during the crucial period from 1930 to 1960. Apparently Burt was not above altering some of his measurements, and possibly even inventing imaginary co-workers, to support his claims. It is hard to know the extent to which this invalidates the main body of his work; but the revealing thing is that the man whose research was held up as a notable example of what the science of the person should be, was not a neutral, detached observer after all; there were certain 'facts' which he wished to prove. Whatever may be said about his measurements, it means that his numerous comments on the educational scene, many of which have formed the cornerstone of policy decisions, must be viewed with great suspicion. And if Burt, who had such high standards in many aspects of his work, has been found to be fallible, what about the hundreds of others, much smaller in stature as persons, who have been involved in similar research?

The main thrust of our argument, however, is not to point out that certain psychologists and others have failed to conform to the standards which they officially upheld for scientific work. Even if not a single measurement had been faked, the basic point we are trying to make would stand. It is that there is something seriously and sadly wrong with the whole approach. Anyone who tries to take the position of an uninvolved, detached observer, apparently without values or commitments, can understand very little about social processes. The parts which can be measured are often relatively trivial; many aspects of what it is to be human will be ignored, and sooner or later the researcher's hidden values will show through.

Education, as an activity, cannot be studied in this way. For here we are dealing with human beings in their growth as persons; the basic presupposition of the whole enterprise is that they are not static beings with fixed attributes. It is during the process of education that part of the formation of persons occurs, with the aim that ultimately they should learn to take the responsibility for the forming of themselves. Thus to measure the person in simplistic ways, as we have done in Britain for over 30 years, and to formulate policy on the basis of such measurement, is counter-educational. We believe that in the long run, the consequences of this will be a drastic *fall* in standards, not only in schools, but also in social, industrial and political life. For the simple fact is that we can't separate education from society, or society from the individuals who make it up.

5. Education is about People

In a way this seems so obvious, and in our saner moments we all know it. The whole business of teaching and learning is an activity of people trying to relate to one another, helping each other to develop their many faculties. It can have a significance and satisfaction for all. This is far more important than classrooms, curricula, time-tables, equipment, registers, dinner money, and all the rest of the paraphernalia of school. It is also more important than processing people for places at work; the essentials of most jobs are learned on the job, or in a specialist training. Education is to help us function as fully as possible — as human beings.

Now the curious fact is that the present controversy about standards, and the style of educational research which has brought matters to a head, overlooks these simple points. In the whole debate there has been no serious attempt to consider what it means to be a person. The teacher is viewed as a kind of characterless supervisor, one who practices a certain 'style'; the pupil is viewed as a robot, exhibiting certain 'behaviours', and with a 'progress' to be assessed. It has been rightly said that the main tradition in educational research is more suited for plants than people; as a matter of fact it was in botany that many of the statistical methods did originate! In the current controversy policy-makers, politicians, and researchers are recognised as persons. But the rest — teachers and children alike — are regarded virtually as measurable objects, and of a very simple kind.

If we wish to live in a society of real humanity, this sort of slipshod thinking won't do. Every person is unique. We cannot crudely lump teachers together according to their 'style', or pupils by their responses to very simple 'personality' questionnaires. There's much more difference between people than that. Here are a few illustrations of what this means.

We know, for a start, that each person looks at the same situation differently. One child may dread the classroom, while another faces learning with confidence.

One may come well-fed and eager to take part; another may be looking forward to school dinner as the first proper meal of the day. One may find school a happy relief from the tensions of home; another may find home a refuge from the friendlessness of school. One child may see the teacher as a kindly aunt; another, as a remote figure who cannot understand. The same kind of thing applies to teachers; some may look on their work as a vocation, and the classroom as a place of fulfilment; others may see teaching as something to be got through before real life begins at four o'clock.

There is also the question of motives. It is not simply a matter of what a person says and does, but of reasons for action. We all recognise that effectiveness in teaching is related in some way to having a genuine concern for children, to commitment to the job, including the chores. No amount of technique (important though that is), can compensate for lack of caring. Going a little deeper, there may be many reasons for adopting a particular 'style'. One teacher might become a rigid authoritarian because of a secret fear or envy of children and their spontaneity, or simply because of a delight in dominating the powerless. Another might prefer to be 'progressive' because it can be a soft option, allowing the teacher never to prepare a lesson or to look at the work a child has done. One teacher may be at the disposal of others; another might have so many personal problems that it is impossible to give full attention to the needs of other people.

It seems obvious that a caring, experienced teacher's 'style' will have components of traditional and progressive, discipline and permissiveness, routine and variety — and that the dominance of any aspect will be geared to the demands of the situation. This will take account of numerous factors, including the needs of the children, the type of lesson material — even the time of the day! But it will contain a further crucial component — and that is respect for the children as persons.

Children have their motives too. If a child seeks attention it may be because of a liking for the teacher; but it could be because there is not enough attention at home. If a child becomes a model pupil it may be because of a genuine love of learning; but it could be that the human task of making friendships is too hard. One child may disrupt the class because it is not sufficiently challenging, while another may do much the same because of a fear of being shown up as a slow learner. Indeed, all simple classifications of children's behaviour are dubious. Even fidgeting could mean many things: boredom, anxiety, extreme concentration, excess of physical energy, tiredness — or wanting to go to the lavatory.

There's another thing we can't ignore without grossly misunderstanding what goes on in classrooms. It is the fact that being human means being in relationships. As every good teacher knows, children are involved in an ever-changing network of friendships among themselves, the pattern changing almost from day to day. And each one has a unique quality of relationship with the teacher (insofar as our absurd under-staffing allows it at all). Children are in many ways excellent psychologists, often more sensitive than professional observers. They perceive from many subtle cues whether they are liked and their viewpoint respected. They come to know what is expected of them, what kind of eccentricities are acceptable, what they can and cannot get away with. Thus the classroom is not, primarily, a place of 'styles', 'standards', and 'behaviours'. It is a place where people are working out a way of living together; what goes on there sooner or later affects human relationships in society as a whole.

Children in school learn a great deal about themselves. From what they are taught (and the way they are taught it), from their relationships, from the way they are treated and reacted to, children learn what is known as the 'hidden curriculum'. They learn what kind of person they are, and their place in life; they learn whether or not they are 'worthwhile' people. And this is why respect for children as persons is such an important aspect of the teacher's role. For if this respect is not present, it will be apparent to the children — and may have both deep and lasting consequences.

It is not too far-fetched to suggest that to be a success in the British Education System is to have learned to be individualistic and competitive — to have learned to measure one's success not simply in terms of personal progress or development, but also in terms which make reference to others' failure.

This kind of thinking is well illustrated in wider society, where a lack of concern for others is more generally apparent than is mutual caring, cooperation or community feeling. Is it not at least possible that an emphasis on cooperation instead of competition in our primary schools could go at least some way towards creating a more genuinely human and caring (as well as intelligent) society? There are, after all, other cultures in the world (ironically often regarded as 'primitive') where genuine cooperation is a central value. There are no grounds for accepting that self-interest must be a key factor in human social existence.

Then we must remember that human beings have the capacity for growth and development. Whatever may be the truth on the question of 'innate ability' (and at present no-one knows), it is beyond dispute that many of the children in our schools are performing far below their potential. Much the same could also be said of teachers. They do not simply adopt a 'style' and keep it, but are constantly changing what they do in the light of growing confidence and experience. Many of them, too, have potential yet to be fulfilled. To regard people as having a fixed quantity of personality and ability fits very well the view of education as a way of allocating trained workers into slots in the social system. It is, however, neither true nor just.

You may well ask, then, whether it is possible to carry out 'scientific' and 'objective' research at all in the area of teaching and learning. Some of the most important factors are those which cannot be 'measured' at all. To this there is one very simple answer. Any kind of research which claims to be scientific and neglects such aspects of the person as we have discussed here is a fraud. It simply isn't 'true to life', and so fails to meet the first requirement of a science. It would be about as absurd as to propose theories about the circulatory system and deliberately ignore, for the sake of simplicity of measurement, the fact that the heart acts as a pump and the blood moves through the arteries!

The debate about standards has time and again involved similar errors. It has forgotten what it means to be human, and overlooked the wider purpose of education. The same might be said about much of the research which has been cited as 'evidence'. If we want simply to manipulate people, to perpetuate the longstanding inadequacies of the education system, a discussion at this level will do admirably. But it will not do if our aim is a deeper understanding, and the continued improvement of our primary schools.

Actually, it *is* possible to do research which can claim to be scientific, which takes 'being human' seriously. There have been many examples in other fields, and of course a number within education too. Generally, though, they don't hit the headlines. A more human type of research tends to be cautious about making sweeping generalisations, and often its aim is to shed light rather than to make bold predictions. We would do well here to carry out an inquiry into excellence in teaching, and perhaps even start with that one teacher who stood out in the Bennett Report. Such a piece of research, which would cost far less than any 'improved' version of that carried out by the Lancaster team, would probably yield a rich harvest of insight which could be passed on to teachers and those at present in training. Its results would certainly be more valuable — and more human — than those which emerge from the accepted form of research.

But all this raises a further question, which is the crux of the whole debate. Suppose that we did find how to bring about great improvements in our primary schools, including how to raise the national standards in literacy and numeracy to vastly higher levels than they are now. What, in the long run, would be the point? Almost everyone seems to believe that there would be one. We do, too. But this requires us to think clearly and seriously about what we are really trying to do in education, both for individuals and for society.

6. Education - for What?

The claims of this booklet thus far can be summed up in seven simple points. First, while primary schools must maintain high standards of literacy and numeracy, these are not the only things that matter. Second, it is unrealistic and unhelpful to force a division between 'traditional' and 'progressive', as rival styles of education. Third, the debate about standards is part of a much larger issue, from which it cannot be separated. Fourth, our judgement must take into account the long-term educational history of Britain, looking both back into the past and forward into the future. Fifth, the research which has been cited by those who cry out for a return to the old ways is unsound, even by its own standards. Sixth, the debate, including the research, has generally been carried out on a false basis, because it has forgotten the most important element — people. Seventh, education must be seen not as a factory for producing exam passes, but as a means for enabling people to live more fully human lives.

Now the argument must be pressed further. We must face the vital question of the broader purpose of education in relation to society, both now and in the future. For it is not just an individual matter; education and society affect one another constantly, and sometimes in powerful ways. Here, perhaps, the controversy over standards has reached its highest level of confusion. Probably we all realise, if dimly, that Britain is still a society with great inequalities, inherited from the past. This is true on an individual level, but also for whole social groups. If we compare, say, the life-prospects of solicitors with those of unskilled labourers in the chemical industry, the point is immediately clear. There are vast differences between the various sectors of society, extending over virtually every aspect of life — and death. The statistics, which are well documented, tell their own story. A person's chances of surviving at birth, of receiving adequate and timely medical care, of moving easily through the educational system, of remaining employed, of avoiding insanity (or being well cared for when insane), of having a pension, of living to a ripe old age, are all related to social class. This is not simply a matter of income, status, power, or wealth, though these are included. Fundamentally, the quality of life is at stake.

It is, of course, the job a person does which mainly determines lifestyle. It is the education which mainly determines the job. And it is the social background (in other words, the lifestyle of the parents) which mainly determines the education. Of course there are exceptions, the success-stories which seem to reassure us that our society provides the means of advancement to everyone. These, however, are conspicuously rare. The main fact is that we have a social system which inexorably seems to reproduce itself. Education is one of the main means by which it does so.

People sometimes talk as if Britain were gradually becoming a classless society. This is largely a fiction, as the statistics make very plain. It is easy to draw false conclusions here, on the basis of casual impressions. Indeed, it is very difficult for anyone to gain a balanced picture of the whole of society, because we all tend to gather among people of our own kind; our friends are generally like ourselves. Unless we make a very deliberate effort to find out the truth, other parts of the social system remain hidden from us. Of course some of the centres of power and wealth in that system have shifted to some extent. There is, however, little indication that we have gone very far towards creating a society with genuinely human prospects for all.

Teachers, probably more than most, are aware of the divisions and inequalities which surround us. They know that education provides the main tickets to success, and therefore what power and responsibility are in their hands. They may well feel that the main way they can help their pupils on to a 'better' life is by getting them through exams: for some this is the main expression of their caring. If they can convince themselves that they have gone some way towards providing equality of opportunity to school children, they can feel slightly more comfortable when faced with the disheartening reality of a social system which is a society only in name.

There is a fatal flaw, though, in this way of thinking, if everyone were to adopt it. The number of privileged jobs in any country is strictly limited; schools have no direct effect on the structure of opportunity. Suppose, then, we could wave a magic wand and turn all today's academic failures into tomorrow's successes, what would be the result? Society would not change so as to create privileged positions for all who had then achieved the necessary qualifications. Universities, colleges and employers would simply raise or alter their bases of selection, so that there would again be the right number of people to fill the posts. The rest would still be the failures, at a higher educational level.

The realistic conclusion, then, is this. As long as we live in a country where access to advantage is via educational qualifications, education as a means to that end can only benefit the few, never the many. Under this arrangement schools are bound to confer the label of failure on the majority of children, in the process of enabling a few to succeed. It seems likely that the loss of zest for living and learning which occurs in many during their 11 or so years at school is partly the result of this fact. Children from all social backgrounds show great promise at 5 or 6 years old. Somewhere, en route to adulthood, their potential becomes lost or deeply hidden. Many of those who are on the way to acquiring the 'failure' label are psychologically 'camping' at school, accepting it sullenly or with defiance, truanting when they can or dare, and waiting day by day for the farce to end.

This might appear a depressing and inevitable picture, but it need not necessarily be so. We ought always to remember that social structures are man-made, not God-given: they *are* amenable to change. To bring this about on a large scale will require understanding, persistence and moral courage.

One radical change of attitude is required. We should look on the future, not from the narrow vantage-point of personal gain, but considering society as a whole. This is difficult for parents, because naturally they want the best possible foundation for life for their children. It is often hard for teachers, too, who are eager that their own pupils should get as much as they can from the opportunities education provides. But this, by itself, is shallow thinking. On the present system, if one child is an educational success, four others will be failures; if the children in one class do well, the price will be that others have done badly. The same system that makes some, breaks others.

In the long run, however, the successes and the failures will have to live side by side. Judging by the last hundred years, and the state of the country at present, this is not a satisfying or harmonious form of social existence. If we perpetuate it for our children, strife will certainly continue, and democracy itself may well collapse.

So it is essential that we change our view of education, and see it as serving a larger and more human purpose. It must be something for every person, a means towards the unfolding of the abilities which they undoubtedly have. Education is not just about 'standards', as narrowly conceived. It is about the natural world, about human relationships, about social responsibility, about culture, about responding to the wonder of being alive. Of course, amongst this, both literacy and numeracy are important. But it would be sadly mistaken to see them as merely part of the technique for gaining personal advantage, or as tools of the trade in a complex technological society. Institutions exist for people, and not the other way round.

So our schools must not be allowed to be no more than heartless academic factories, turning out people dominated by self-interest, as has so often happened in the past. This is why we have stressed the need to see the current debate in a broad context — and this includes an historical one. For the controversy about falling standards seems to be taking us in the direction of a system which contains remarkable similarities to the very early days of 'universal' education. When the notion of education for one's station in life was replaced by some notion of equality of opportunity, the way to achieve this was seen as being via a national core curriculum (the 3 R's) and by nationally implemented testing procedures. Under this system, school classes were 'inspected' to ensure that the children had 'attained' to a certain level — and if they hadn't their teachers were deemed to be failures.

Now, at first glance, this does not seem to be a

totally unreasonable situation. But a moment's thought tells us, as it told eminent educationalists of the day, that the consequences of such a system are purely mechanical learning on the part of the children, and purely mechanical (rote or drill techniques) on the part of the teachers. Little 'real' learning takes place in this kind of situation, although it was, and is, relatively easy to train children to pass tests in a 'parrot-type' fashion. Yet this is the kind of farcical situation to which the Black Paper writers would have us return; this is the kind of situation to which certain politicians would have us return. But now they do this by reference to 'scientific' research, and in the name of equality and objectivity.

And the real tragedy is that the present educational system contains many promising signs. Some of our schools are becoming centres of community, serving not only children, but people of all ages. Library facilities are being used more. There is an increased demand among young and old for education which is not geared to exams and qualifications. There is greater parental and community involvement with schools than there ever has been in the past. There are some indications of increased social and political concern, and of a greater sense of caring among young people. It is quite false to claim that these work against high academic standards. There is now, throughout the country, a higher level of education than there has been at any other period.

Putting it another way, it is the dominant conception of human worth — at present accepted by many of the 'failures' as well as the 'successes' — which must be altered. In our traditions we lay stress on individual competition and put people into rank orders. We implicitly teach that possessing much and consuming more are the outstanding human achievements. Now is the time for the focus of our education to be placed elsewhere: on co-operating with others, being creative, caring, joyful, making the most of the conditions of life. Of course we need people to carry forward our industrial and commercial effort, but industry and commerce need humanity too.

And the point that must be stressed again is that none of this implies a lowering of standards in any sense at all; if anything it implies a much higher — though broader — conception of standards. But the widespread belief in our society that we can, and should, rank people according to their performance on so-called 'objective' tests tends to mitigate against this broader conception of standards, talent and general human worth. Here we would make two points. The first is that our ability to measure intelligence, 'talent' and even attainment, is far more limited than some people would have us believe. The second is quite simply that even if we had perfected the techniques required to measure such aspects of persons, would we really wish for a society dominated by the 'able' as measured only by such tests? Would we really want all our decisions to be made by people who scored highly on so-called intelligence tests, with no reference to qualities of personality, humanity and so on?

The relevance of this to our education system in general, and to the heated debate about standards lies in the fact that testing and measurement seem to be accepted as being the 'right' and 'proper' way of going about things. Our secondary education sector, in general, is dominated by exams which make reference to the concept of intelligence. Now it seems that our primary sector is to be 'brought back into line' — it was apparently straying too far away from routine testing as a means of assessing children's ability and attainment. The threat of a reactionary, retrograde movement is a very real one. The recommendations of the Black Paper writers for national testing at prescribed stages have been accepted. One of the editors of these publications has received 'formal' recognition at Central Political Party level; and the education system is characterized by increasing bureaucracy at all levels and in all forms. The wheel appears to have turned full-circle. The only 'basic' difference between the modern call for maintaining standards by regular testing, and that same call nearly 100 years ago, is that we now have bigger and better tests. But what *kind*? Tests to process people more accurately and efficiently?

The world is changing, whether we like that fact or not. It is time for us to take responsibility for change, and turn it to the social good. There can be little doubt that during the next decade hours of work will become shorter and retirement will generally be younger. There will be less work for society to share around. If we hold onto the conception of education which is built into our history it means that large parts of life are going to be very empty for many people. The message we have inherited is outmoded and unjust. "To the many — education for drudgery; to the few — education for power." This must now be replaced by a different message, the one to which so many of the positive changes in our schools have been pointing. "To all of society — education for life."

7. Looking to the Future

The controversy over standards has now gone on for some time, and during 1975 and 1976 there were points where it almost reached hysteria level. But it would be a mistake to assume that a period of relative quiet indicates that the matter is closed. All that has happened so far may well prove to have been only the beginning of the great debate. In the present climate of despondency anything could happen; just as there has been a blind rush to blame education for some of our social ills, there may well be precipitate changes of policy. As we look ahead, here are four suggestions which might help turn to good effect a debate which could otherwise be very harmful to the cause of justice and sanity in State Education.

First, we should reject any assertions that it has been proved, through scientific investigation, that 'progressive educational methods' are inferior. There isn't any one thing which can be called 'progressive', or which can be called 'traditional'; and when such concepts are bandied around by politicians or the news media they serve to arouse emotion, but not clear thinking. In the realities of the school it is just not possible to use such labels, since there are so many aspects to teaching and learning. By all means let's discuss methods of teaching reading, the layout of the classroom, forms of discipline, the broader aims of primary education, and so on, but let's not carry out so significant a debate by making a crude polarization of opinion. There are probably very few teachers who would happily accept the label 'traditional' or 'progressive', and few schools to which such simple terms could properly apply. The whole debate has done a great disservice to educational thought by reducing the issues to the level of deceptive jargon.

Once a piece of information that accords with widespread anxiety has been lodged in people's minds it is extremely hard to remove it. However, an informed minority can do much to counteract bogus assertions, and make clear to other people what the issues really are. As in so many similar situations, those with vested interests have an over-simple case to put forward, and can operate with slogans. They can easily make an impact on the public whose thinking moves quickly from one fragment of information to the next. Counter-arguments are harder to put forward, because they require careful thought. The view we are commending here is considerably more intricate than the reactionary cry of "Return to 3 R's", but it is not unduly complex. By spreading a reasoned view as widely as possible among parents, teachers, and all who are concerned, we can slowly undo the damage that has been done during the last few years.

Second, we should do all that we can to oppose political pressure which uses research findings out of context, and without careful examination of their validity. An immense amount of research has been done over the last 20 years or so, some of it brilliant, some of it appallingly naive. The collection of 'findings', full of mutual contradictions, lies around like a vast heap of spare parts. Every now and again a piece is put onto the heap which exactly matches what a policy-maker or politician 'wants to know', so he pulls it out and makes use of it for his particular purpose. This, it seems, is what has happened with the Bennett Report. We should look with suspicion on the way it has been exploited. Almost always, when a large-scale controversy is aroused, as a consequence of research, it means that vested interests are at stake.

Pressure is to be resisted in two main ways; by knowledge and by counter-pressure. If this booklet has provided the basic information to help you to understand the significance of the debate over standards, it will have succeeded in its aims. But there are several active ways, too, in which we can be involved in bringing pressure to bear. For example, there may be an opportunity to use the public media. Schools have their boards of managers or governors, and we can approach them. Through local councillors and M.P.'s we can help to ensure that needs are met and abuses rectified. Within the teaching profession itself it is noteworthy that the unions have done a great deal to protect their members with regard to pay and conditions of work. How about working through the unions on behalf of school-children, too? There are aspects of their lives at school, such as *their* conditions of work, and the allocation of resources on *their* behalf, which could well be viewed as being within the scope of union concern. Perhaps the most important thing of all at this stage is that we should press for more information. Although our society claims to be democratic, many decisions are taken in a very undemocratic way — and there are many examples of this process operating in the sphere of education. In the long run we want to see schools serving the needs of those who go to them, and not the alleged needs of society, or industry, which all too often really means the needs of those in power.

Third, we would do well to think critically about what we are hoping to do for children by submitting them to the process we call education. What kind of persons do we want, and what kind of society are we hoping for? If you have simple answers here it almost certainly means that you have not thought the matter through, or examined basic assumptions. We are all products of schools, so we tend to take their existence for granted and rarely question their aims. And although this may not be a popular assertion, the fact must be faced that all education is political, in what it does and does not do for people, in what it says and does not say. If you have regarded it as an activity on its own, separate from society, we hope that you will think again. What is happening *now,* to the children who are at school, is preparing the way for the society in which they will live as adults. For this reason, 'standards' can never be simply a matter of academic concern. If an understanding of the social and historical issues involved is lacking, there is the possibility that people will be taken in by the kind of emotive arguments that have been used. They might find themselves pressing for measures which would destroy the very things they believe in — and this would be done with the best of intentions.

The real division, we suggest, is not between supporters of 'traditional' and of 'progressive' education. It is between those who are wearing blinkers and those who have a concern for the whole fabric of social life. The former sometimes appear to have a reassuring message, of rightness and goodness, because they appeal to what is familiar and therefore less feared. It is here that we should think again. The latter group are sometimes accused of being irresponsible, because their concern makes them believe that we could be doing something better. But it is true that some, at least, of the injustices of our society can be remedied through the education system — some have been already, and more can be done if we have the will.

We should insist on the highest possible standards in all aspects of our educational system. Like Black Paper No. 5, this booklet also calls to "all politicians, parents, and teachers to be absolutely intransigent about fundamentals", and appeals to parents to "Apply pressure on your local school to maintain standards . . . Demand higher standards of behaviour at school." But we have defined the principal terms differently. *The fundamentals* involve people's total life-prospects, not just the exams they pass. *Academic standards* of course includes the 3 R's, but these are only part of something much greater. *Standards of behaviour* not only means respect from children to teachers, but also the other way round, both at the personal level and in our social planning.

Because of an outlook which is too narrow in its subject-matter and too limited in its scope, there is the likelihood that many people could press for measures which would in the long run destroy the very things they believe in: and they would do so with the best of intentions. They might even be unwitting agents in the maintaining of injustices in our society at the very time when these can be remedied. That is why we must think clearly. Our educational system is still open to creative change, but it may not always be so.

Finally, we should insist on the highest possible standards, in all aspects of primary education. There can be no doubt that over our long history, and for various different reasons, schools have failed to meet the needs of many children. Sometimes there *has* been a neglect of those basic skills in numeracy and literacy on which so much else is founded. More often the broader education of children, which can enrich their whole response to being alive, has been forgotten. Part of the failure has been ignorance, part idleness, part human inadequacy, part because we have been through a period of very rapid change. Now, however, the situation is settling down again. Despite the prospect of less books and equipment, and despite the ratio of pupils to teachers being much higher than is desirable, the situation is full of promise. We could now make great progress, and do better than we have ever done before, for children from every kind of background.

Where schools are not doing their job properly, we should insist that they take themselves in hand. The means of making complaint, and of insisting on investigation into incompetence are available. Teachers cannot be allowed to shift the blame onto the homes when children fail. There is a wealth of skill and understanding in our heritage; it is up to the schools to draw on this for the benefit of all.

So a great opportunity is upon us, and the controversy over standards reveals how significant it is. Here we have a task to face, whether we are parents, teachers, or concerned onlookers in this debate. We must neither abuse nor negate our responsibility, however much the odds seem to be stacked against us. Children are in no position to fight for their rights as human beings: we are. And one of the most basic of these is the right to a good education.

Other titles available from Writers & Readers ...

After Deschooling What? by Ivan Illich, introduced by Ian Lister
p/b 35p ISBN 0 904613 36 4

Imprisoned in the Global Classroom by Ivan Illich and Etienne Verne
p/b 45p ISBN 0 904613 30 5

Education: The Practice of Freedom by Paulo Freire
p/b £1.00 ISBN 0 904613 16 X

William Tyndale: The Teachers' Story by Terry Ellis, Jackie McWhirter, Dorothy McColgan, Brian Haddow
p/b £1.00 ISBN 0 904613 31 3

Words: as Definitions of Experience by Arnold Wesker ... extending the debate on literacy; the celebrated dramatist proposes an exciting new classroom subject. An appended essay by Richard Appignanesi discusses the relevancy of Wesker's work to Freire's concept of cultural literacy.
p/b 75p ISBN 0 904613 26 7

... and forthcoming titles for '77

The World in a Classroom compiled by Chris Searle ... a powerful new compilation of children's writings which combats racism in the classroom.
p/b £1.95 ISBN 0 904613 46 1 h/b £4.95 ISBN 0 904613 45 3

The Politics of Literacy edited by Martin Hoyles ... finally! a basic literacy reader. Literacy examined in the contexts of race, sex, class and culture, history and ideology.
p/b £1.50 ISBN 0 904613 28 3 h/b £3.95 ISBN 0 904613 47 X

Order from your bookshop or direct from:

Writers and Readers Publishing Cooperative, 14 Talacre Road, London NW5 3PE